# Living the Verb



Fay L. Loomis

ISBN: 978-93-6354-913-5

First Edition: 2025
Rs. 200/-

Cyberwit.net
HIG 45 Kaushambi Kunj, Kalindipuram
Allahabad - 211011 (U.P.) India
http://www.cyberwit.net
E-mail: info@cyberwit.net



Printed at Repro.

# Contents

# Tending Garden

my garden is shifting
I'm unsure what will thrive

well watered, over watered
too much light, not enough

I must select mindset well
not too picky, not too flaccid

consciously cultivate
live the verb

# I Celebrate Me

87 years of age
limited by stroke
cold tugging me down

honey calms ragged cough
long for soak in bath
shampoo

surprise myself by getting dressed
rather than fresh pajamas
even slip on shoes

settle into a soft chair
start another novel

# Apple

red and gold
variegated globe

slice in half
draw quarters

dip in salt
bitter and sweet

# Inexhaustible Gifts

wolf bites butt
pry jaws open
swallow
whole

drink bitter cup
regurgitate darkness
holy light
reveals

# Sady

There once was a lady named Sady
Her daddy eclipsed it to Tady

She hated his slip
Even more his lip

And slugged him right into Hades

# Metamorphosis

*In Memoriam: Joan Miller Bladden*

where are you
dear sister
frozen bird
afraid to sing

in death
you open
your throat
fly

# Sacred

snakes of fire writhe
smoke chokes my nostrils

my beloved mountains
scarred black

# Then I Will Know

cold breeze blows
across doorway

north wind
brittle heart breath

when I let in warmth
then I will know

# Acknowledgments

I am grateful to the editors of the publications in which the following poems have or will appear:

"Tending Garden," *Feeding the Holy*, June 23, 2025

"I Celebrate Me," *Magnets and Ladders*, Spring/Summer 2025; *World Insane*, May 28, 2025; *Serendipity Archives*, tba.

"Apple," *Ameythyst Review*, May 19, 2025

"Inexhaustible Gifts," *Rat's Ass Review*, Spring/Summer 2025

"Metamorphosis," *Al-Khemia Poetica*, April 18, 2025

I deeply appreciate the feedback I receive from writers at the Stone Ridge Library Writers and the Rats Ass Review Workshop. Additionally I am indebted to family and friends who over the years continue to support my writing.